From the Ganga to the Tay:

a poetic conversation between the Ganges and the Tay

An epic poem by
BASHABI FRASER

Photographs by KENNY MUNRO
and BASHABI FRASER

Luath Press Limited
EDINBURGH
www.luath.co.uk

First published 2009

ISBN: 978-1-906307-95-0

The author's right to be identified
as author of this book under the
Copyright, Designs and Patents Act
1988 has been asserted.

The publisher acknowledges the
support of

 Scottish
Arts Council

towards the publication of this volume.

The paper used in this book is
recyclable. It is made from
low chlorine pulps produced in a
low energy, low emission manner
from renewable forests.

Printed and bound by
The Charlesworth Group, Wakefield

Design by Tom Bee

Typeset in Mentor by 3btype.com

Poem © Bashabi Fraser 2009

Teachers' notes are available
through Luath Press

To Baba, to whom I owe the privilege of growing up in the land of the Ganga.

To Neil, who introduced me to the beauty of the Tay terrain.

To Rupsha, whose very name is that of a river, and who, in herself, unites the two lands watered by these two historic rivers.

'But pleasures are like poppies spread,
You seize the flower, its bloom is shed;
Or like the snow falls in the river,
A moment white - then melts forever'

Robert Burns, 'Tam O' Shanter'

– While rivers flow on through the ages
Taking note of history's pages...

Acknowledgements

WE WOULD LIKE TO thank all the organisations who have financed us on our trips to India to take the photographs which bring the epic poem *From the Ganga to the Tay* alive. Kenny received grants from the Scottish Arts Council, Aberdeenshire Council, Royal Scottish Geographical Society and the Geddes Trust for his visits to Bengal and I was able to travel to India and along the Ganga with research grants from Napier University and the Carnegie Trust and support from the British Council in Kolkata. Both Kenny and I were warmly looked after in India, so while my aunt, Reba Chakraborty, made my stay anxiety-free and comfortable, Kenny's hosts were his artist friends, Tandra and Pulak Ghosh.

The material in the National Library of Scotland and at Edinburgh University Library has proved an invaluable resource on the history of Indo–Scottish connections.

There were acts of generosity which facilitated the poem, like that of the receptionist at my optician's in Edinburgh, who insisted that I keep an issue of *The Scots Magazine* which had a feature on the Tay. I am grateful to my husband, Neil, and my father, Bimalendu Bhattacharya, for giving me their time and help on my many trips along the Tay over a few years and for accompanying me on the epic journey along the Ganga in July 2008. On this last trip, my cousin, Rajatshuvra Chakraborty, took several of the photographs and helped us with the technology of digital transfer. My father, who is a geographer, also acted as a reference point for checking many geographical details related to the two rivers while I was writing the poem.

I would like to thank many of my writer friends in Scotland and my colleagues at Napier University for their patience in reading through the poem and giving me their insightful comments.

I am grateful to Luath Press for publishing this book which has had a long journey in its making, like the rivers whose story it portrays. Kenny would like to thank Sheena Watson and her daughter, Kerry, for their constant support of the project, helping him on many photo shoots, and for conducting research into the history of Kenny's ancestral links with India. Finally, I am grateful to my family, especially to my daughter, Rupsha, who have all read through several drafts of the poem and have been good sounding boards and encouraging readers.

Bashabi Fraser

Preface

'I am forever restless,
My depths holding the secret of my progress'
(translated from Rabindranath Tagore's song, 'Oh River')

THE STORY OF THIS POEM begins not beside the Ganga or the Tay, but along another river, the Karnaphuli, which leaps from the hills above Rangamati, a beautiful town in Chittagong district. The port of Chittagong has grown on either side of Karnaphuli's banks, just before it flows into the Bay of Bengal. It is this river that was the highway my paternal grandfather used to travel to and from his ancestral village and Chittagong. In this riverine terrain, the arteries of transport were rivers which form a network that connected a fertile land where the British Empire ruled from, in Bengal, till 1911-12, after which the imperial capital moved to Delhi.

However, this story is not about Empire but about an association that grew out of a colonial encounter. My great grandfather worked for a Scots sahib who grew very fond of his bright eyed, gentle, studious son, who was my grandfather, my Dadu, and supervised his studies. By a stroke of ill luck, my great grandfather died when my grandfather was about 12. It was then that the Scottish civil servant took on the full responsibility of Dadu's education and helped him to find a job. When the Scotsman and his wife suggested Dadu come with them when they were returning 'home', Dadu was touched, but he could not leave his widowed mother and felt he had a lot of responsibility still towards his siblings. But the link with Scotland was made and I was to hear this story of the kindly Scotsman and his wife from my Dadu later.

Decades later, when my parents were researchers at the London School of Economics in the '6os, they met Arthur Geddes, the geographer son of the Scots architect and town planner, Patrick Geddes. In London, they also met Julian Dakin the linguist and historian, who became a life-long friend and travelled to work in Kolkata (Calcutta) after my parents returned. When Julian left India, he came to teach at Edinburgh University. He died in 1972 but the fact that his widow, Carmen, still lived in Edinburgh, brought me to the city and to Julian's very Department to work on a section of my PHD thesis in the '80s. By a fortuitous coincidence I met Jeannie Geddes, Arthur Geddes' wife on this visit, who was a friend of Carmen's. Jeannie gave me a copy of Arthur Geddes' translation of Rabindranath Tagore's songs that he had set to music. The thread between Scotland and India was being woven through various family associations and friendships, through time.

I met Neil on my research trip to Scotland and married him on his seventh visit to Kolkata where I had returned to teach; thus my link with Scotland was renewed, my husband's family being descended from the Frasers of Inverness-shire. When I came back to Edinburgh after my marriage, I met Murdo Macdonald, the Scottish Art Historian and Geddesian, who told me of the correspondence between Patrick Geddes and Rabindranath Tagore in the National Library of Scotland and asked me if I could trace the other side of the correspondence. Another Scot, Professor Kitty Datta was Head of English at Jadavpur University in Kolkata, where I had done my Master's degree. Years later, when our paths converged again, this time in Britain, Kitty told me that I should edit the correspondence, which I did. So the magic of Scotland had begun to take hold of me.

Through the years, I have followed the multiple links between Scotland and India and one that has fascinated me was the jute trade route that linked Dundee directly with Kolkata. I saw how the rivers on which these two cities stood played a crucial role in their very foundation and the establishment and continuation of the jute trade. Two years ago, we took a boat trip along the Hugli, a distributary of the Ganga, on which Kolkata stands. On this river journey we saw the string of jute managers' bungalows and of the Indian aristocracy and British administrators aristocratic palaces which stood as a testimony to a city that grew as a result of colonial trade at the focal point of a Ganga estuary.

The story of rivers is the story of the growth of civilisation as people settled along flowing water, which held the promise of a constant source of water for living purposes, irrigating the hinterland, providing hydroelectric power and being an avenue for transport. Rivers provide livelihoods for many, like fishermen, boatmen and traders. There is food in their depths in the fish that find a home in their assured flow. They remain a symbol of life's continuity and a rich source of inspiration for artists and writers.

It was Kenny Munro, who, after his visits to India, told me that he understood how sacred rivers were as that was how they were viewed in India - with reverence and worshipped for their power and generosity. Sometimes when one moves away from one's country, one understands the significance of some of the deep truths and prevailing beliefs that are either overlooked or taken for granted while one lives there. I understood exactly what Kenny meant, as I recalled the millions who wade into the Ganga, offering dawn prayers or floating lamps at dusk. I have also sympathised with the people's protests led by activists like the social worker Medha Patkar and Booker Prize winner, Arundhati Roy, fighting for the millions threatened with displacement by the building of a big dam on the mighty Narmada, to finance the wealthy golden corridor of industry in Gujrat, hundreds of miles away from the state of Madhya Pradesh where the Narmada originates. As a daughter of geographers, I know that it is almost suicidal to play with rivers and building big dams can be dangerous as rivers can change course and be twisted out of existence.

Kenny said that this sense of the river being sacred was something we had lost in the west. But have we? In the west poets have written about rivers, musicians have composed music on them, artists have drawn them and ferries still ply on them. Also, they provide multiple sports, daring the adventurer to their surface and depths. Now, with the threat of global warming being so pressing, river transport and hydroelectricity have been imbued with fresh significance for a viable future. The romance of rivers has a fresh appeal.

Currently, I am working on a project on Scots in India, and once again, I have been swept into the reality of a historic chain of association, and the most striking one remains the golden skein that wove the nations through years of industrial exchange and interdependence. Paddy fields were converted to the lucrative jute fields, and the new crops' lust for huge quantities of water could only be supplied by the numerous distributaries of the bountiful Ganga. The raw material then travelled to the factories on the Tay to be processed into ropes and bales for the world market. With the rise and slump of the jute trade, the fortunes of the two nations were inextricably linked together in a see-saw experience. When the War affected the journey and sale of jute, it became clear that it was more profitable to process the jute where it grew. Scottish engineers set up the jute factories on the shores of Bengal, and Indian engineers came to train in Dundee College.

But the lower reaches of the Ganga would be meaningless without the story of the entire river which drew foreigners to India in the first place, to the world's most fertile river valley, the Indo–Gangetic plain. And the 'silvery Tay' remains that historic source for the many stories of Scots in India and Indians in Scotland. Today Britain supports the Ganga Development Scheme to save this mighty river from pollution, the same concern that moves the Scottish authorities to save the salmon in the depths of the Tay. Now there is renewed interest in the west in the many facilities rivers have to offer in fishing, transport, power and sport. Interestingly, both the Ganga and the Tay have similar trajectories as they flow from the west to the east, and the fact that each is the longest river in her/his respective countries, bind them more closely in their shared history and geography.

The link between India and Scotland runs deep, with layers of history in intermingling waves of connection which have been continuous, like a river, a link which is explored by the rivers who speak to each other across the continents and over centuries – Ganga, the mother goddess and Tay the masculine symbol of Celtic heritage – in *From the Ganga to the Tay* brought visually alive by Kenny Munro's photographs. Like the 'Twa Brigs of Ayr', who talk to each other, the rivers Ganga and Tay converse, as they reminisce on a shared history and observe the reality that confronts them now.

Bashabi Fraser

Introduction

*'My childhood river will always be for me my main impulse
of the life-stream and of the cosmos'*

Sir Patrick Geddes

ONE OF RABINDRANATH TAGORE's poems describes a flotilla of paper
boats inscribed with children's names being launched into a stream.
As the boats become part of the river, passing through its village
communities on a meandering course, each one is hopeful of being
'found' by another child. It is a poem which celebrates universal
values of communication and journeys with profound and ancient
undertones.

But why are we compelled to care about rivers? Are we born with
this consciousness?

We have, after all, evolved in the liquid environment of the womb.
Perhaps that has imbued us with a primordial affinity with water;
an innate connection with the qualities of all aquatic environments.
In this respect we have absorbed shared experiences inherited from
our ancestors.

Rivers have strongly influenced our communities and the formation
of early settlements; and explorers, while terrified by their
expeditions, have tingled with excitement when 'crossing water'.
I believe there had once been a more profound cultural attachment
to Scottish rivers, such as the Tay, similar to the daily human
immersions and annual water festivals still taking place along the
Ganges today. Our ancestors have left clues of habitation, journeys,
pilgrimages and conflict such as the ruined abbey at Balmerino,
near the Tay mouth, the ancient canoes discovered at Perth and the
crannogs of Loch Tay. Romans, Vikings and Normans all left their
mark, propagating cultural exchange and trading via the Scottish
rivers. However, recent challenging climatic conditions have forced
this generation to look afresh at our rivers.

From the Ganga to the Tay is a symbolic journey along the River
Ganges and the River Tay from source to sea. It stimulates issues
surrounding our perception and affinity with rivers and the role
they have played in our society. The real and mythical dialogues

within the poem form the basis of an 'ecological echo' which can be heard around the world, revealing an almost timeless relationship between rivers.

The 'conversation' reveals a contemporary questioning edge, yet it also recalls ancient parables, many of which are alluded to on Pictish symbols carved in stone.

The poem is a poignant joining of these two iconic rivers of the world. I was first introduced to Bashabi Fraser in 1998. Since then, the relationship formed and the personal journeys made by Bashabi and myself have converged to form a kind of visual poetry which is as much a catalyst to stimulate discussion as it is a dialogue between the two rivers. Travelling to India several times has enabled me to start to consider the differences between the two rivers; comparing the deep connection between people and river along the banks of the Ganges with that along the banks of the Tay.

I recently discovered an East India company coin dated 1832, which inspired me to research my family history, and found that two of my ancestors lived in India in the mid 19th century. Private James Blacklaw and his wife Janet Binnie, my great-great-grandparents, travelled from Stirling to India with the 42nd (Royal Highland) Regiment of Foot, the 'Black Watch', in 1862. Their first daughter was born near Rawalpindee in 1865 and they returned to Edinburgh in 1868, disembarking at Burntisland. The photos reflect this personal journey and celebrate the rich cultural connections between India and Scotland.

Kenny Munro

GANGA:[1] *They call me Ganga.*
The story of my birth
is a glorious myth.
I am a dream
of Lord Shiva's[2]
rising as a stream.
My tandava –
a liquid secret still
splurging from
his knotted hair.
My feminine will
released to roam
beyond this snowy lair.
While the Destroyer
sleeps,
his latent power
leaps
into my cascades
bidding me go forth
and multiply,
gushing through decades
from the vast north
through flattened plains
down to my Bay.

What do they
call you?
On which day
were you
conceived?

TAY: *My Celtic caves*
heaved
as Nordic waves
received
the omen of my
birth
even before
they set out
for my shores
as Thor[3]

and Odin[4]
would ordain
in years to come.
They call me the Tay.
The truth
is, I too have a bay –
my Firth.
I have this isthmus
of an island
to cross.

But yours is the earth
where I would not be you –
a sub-continent spread out
for your good
or your ill will
to brazenly toss in.

This too is north
but further north than you.

They have laid out
their broad hills
for me to encircle
and cut through
spilling over
rocky beds
under heights
so ancient and wise,
weathered to gentleness
unlike the heady rise
of your stately but
youthful fold mountains.[5]

GANGA: Yes, it was there
where I awoke
to provoke
the world
to my capacious flow.
When I left Shiva's
coiled tresses

for mortals,
I percolated
in diverse
drops of frozen tears
in the portals
of gigantic caves
where my waves
vibrated
at Gangotri.
That too is north
beyond the Garhwal
Hills,[6] the rest is no myth
as I tumble forth
in a mighty torrent
that rents the sky,
rushing down
in sheer abandon,
having forgotten
my frozen foetal
beginnings
in the swirling ice
cold tears
of Bhagirati's[7]
streaming eyes.

TAY: Hush, it is now my turn.
There is no rush
for we have courses
to run
at our own pace.
Let this not be a race
to be done or won -
I too have my
watery womb
suspended high
above sea level
to which others roam,
paying court
at my door -
the Fillan,

the Dochart
and Lochay
who glide
to my side
joining me
on my way.
But I'm not
to be won
by their
supplication.
Theirs is only to
pay homage,
to woo me
night and day,
trying to mingle
their kisses
and caresses
with my tide
and shingle –
aiming to shine
in reflected glory.
But I refrain
from weakening
to flattery.
I was born
to widen and deepen
my goal
and reign.
I am utterly
committed to
my role –
ignoring my importunate
rivals,
heeding instead
imploring and unfortunate
mortals,
spreading my bed
of old,
for their good
and gain.

GANGA: *So have they*
swarmed
to your banks?
Have they
roamed with your stream?
Have they realized dreams
in tune with your whims –
where you curved
or cradled
as you swerved
Or lingered?
Have they come
to build homes
to rest
as your guest
for some scores
of years
on your shores?

TAY: *Aye, at intervals*
along my
hundred and
twenty miles of
serpentine
riverine progress –
they have built
their steeples
and spires
as they live,
and, aspire –
itinerant souls
on my eternal shore –
but their numbers
are few
compared to those
who clamber
at your door.

GANGA: 'Aye', that is
a word
I have heard
spoken
by your countrymen.
I like it, so
I'll use it
to answer
your question –
aye, my people
come in swarms
like summer bees
drawn by promises
of warmth and wealth
to be gathered
with armful ease

But as I have
a sub-continent
to play in
I have ample time
to display
my immensity
and fame.
I cause havoc
I cause pain
I send shocks
of lightning rain
I fan out
my seething wrath
a hooded cobra
hissing death.
My passions churn –
in fierce upsurge
I woo
fortune
and urge
a brooding heaven
to war.

For mine
is the triple path
of heaven,
earth and sea.
The icicles
of Gomukh
could not
bind me
in Shiva's
tangled locks.
Riding on Makara[8]
I flashed
with chameleon
deftness and speed -
from statuesque anchor
to fluid
abandon.
I plunged
in cobalt and white
splendour
to Gauri Kund -
that meditative lake
overlooked
by the ardour
of a temple
built for me
at Gangotri.[9]

Like you,
I have homage
paid by Jadganga
and Kshurganga-[10]
their drainage
and names
borrowed from
my matrilineal heritage.

TAY: *You are proud*
but so am I
with all the obeisance
and offering
endorsing our
very sway
over an unresisting
landmass
which we erode
not with explosions
of cannon or dynamite
but with the might
of fluid gentleness
and tearful coercion.

GANGA: *But men too*
can force nature.
Your men came
to my valleys
and found adventure.
My sheer paddy
green was torn
away and in its
place was sown
a low caste seed,
from which was born
these tall rough
stems which would
hide tigers if
they could,
only tigers don't
prowl here
where this hemp
grows. You may
think my thirst
is great, but you
haven't seen the worst.
My rice beds
stood ankle deep,

apologetic and shy,
their bodies
respectably dry
in my canalled
waters, while only
their ankles stood
lapped over by
a million kisses
of a multitude
of droplets
cradled in square fields
of translucent green
fulfilment.
But these new brazen
Amazons stand waist
deep, like shameless
women in wet saris,
the water cradling
their tilting breasts.

TAY: And does that not
please you, to have
erotic images
livening your journey?

GANGA: But these are crops
not rows of women
in warm and soft
flesh, adorning
the land I drain.
Why, is that what
you would have on your
banks, turning from the dry
mundane to the blushing hot
passion of revealing thighs
and bobbing breasts?

TAY: Aye, I too have
had my hedges

[23]

parted in days of old
  when a Highland lad
  and his blue-eyed
  lass came to my edge
  to bathe on a
    soft dewy spring morning
    and voyeuristic
    I watched –
      and more, I lapped
        them in my arms
        and fashioned
          love's course
          curling round their
          bodies and tumbling
          them together
in sure union.

GANGA: *Ah, but those*
            days are gone;
              you now have laws
                about bathing
                  while I have none.
                    To bathe in me is
                    sacred. I wash
                      their sins away
                    and bring
                    earthly bliss.

            They come with
              their trust
              and stand
              statuesque in
              the beautiful
              half dusk,
              floating lamps,
              sprinkling petals,
            or in the glimmer
            of that first glow
            that defines
              the horizon

at dawn
they come to bestow
their sorrows
in my eternal flow.
Clad in their damp
folds, they mutter
incessant prayers
that tremble and ripple
my middle course,
which sends them
back to Gangotri
and Bhagirati,
knowing they will
penetrate the still
centre of Shiva's
consciousness
to awaken and bless
them in their
deepest distress.

TAY: *What is this 'half*
dusk' you talk of?

GANGA: *It is the time*
when cows return,
raising the dust
in a swirl
of iridescent
vermilion –
the godhuli [11]
– that moment
of semi-secret
light
when brides elect
turn beauty queens
for every groom's
family

            to admire
            and select.

TAY: *Well, I only know the*
            half light of long
                summer days
                    when the sun has
                        left unnoticed –
                        his brightness
                            lingering like a hundred
                        footlights' suffusing
                    beams, their source
                invisible to his audience –
            whose concentrated focus
        is on the lighted ambience
        of this dramatic foray
        marked out with finesse
    in the magic hours
of prolonged daylight –
with the night
    squeezed to a bare
        minimum, by what
        we call twilight.
            So I am there
                visible and outreaching,
                lazily strolling
                    through warm July
                        days, the silent witness
                        to darkness
                            breaching
                            the wee hours wholly
                        but briefly, rolling
                    back again
                as brightness
            reveals my shimmer
        the next dawn.

GANGA: *Twilight sounds like*
            a dream of light –

often imagined
but never happening –
this longed-for delight,
of a day-dream
of sweetness
and infinite light.

TAY: It is no dream
for all the practical
activities of fishing
and sailing, of travel
and business, wishing
continuity and completion,
can find fruition
in my waters'
candid display.
Through calm
September days
of Indian summers –
to borrow a term
from the shy gaze
of your wintry rays
which best describes
these balmy days
moving into a
meditative autumn.

GANGA: My days here are
more dramatic.
Pure gold lines
my shores
before the blazing disc
actually appears.
The ochre orange,
vermilion red,
magenta pink
stroke my sky
and spill across
my expanse

as colours multiply
 and mix,
  vying with my
   upper course silver
    and lower course bronze,
     coppering my
      willing body
       with romance.
        Then I am a
         woman, the sun
         a patriarch,
         no longer dazzled
         by my beauty,
         but desiring
         to command
         and burn my world
        to submission,
       thus weakening
      my will to brim
     and overflow.
    When I am at my lowest
     point from March
      till June, before
       those seasonal winds
        blow my way
         bringing sustenance
         and nourishment
          - the raindrops mingling
          with my steaming tears
         of joy uncompounded
         as my feminine bounty
        finds fulfilment.
       Then my coppery bronze
        surges with teeming
         masses of clouds
          congregating
           in nimbo-stratus
            sheets which canopy
             my horizon.

The sky and I
revel in a shared
camaraderie of abandon
amidst thundering
applause, preceded by
lightning's dazzle.
And when we are spent,
a deep wondering
calm returns
as I find the
sequined velvety
mystery of tropical
moonlight,
when myriad sparkles
gleam and glitter
like a host of
fireflies on my
silvery bangled,
dancing arms
that disarm
my beholders.

TAY: *My Scots travellers*
have written of those
seasonal rains
in letters home,
the Monsoons -
those harbingers
of festive rain
straight from
the mighty main,
the ponderous breast
of the Indian Ocean.
My folk have
marvelled how
you move
from one extreme
to another show -
your parched pain

quenched by such rain!
It is a dream
I seldom see unfold,
for I have my weather,
variable, uncertain,
yet persistent when
it is insistent on
augmenting
my sinuous flow.

GANGA: *But you too*
have your seasons
as your poets
have told mine.
So you have reason
to watch and wait
for winter snow
to melt and divine
clusters of crocuses
to surface and grow,
reminders of change
that ensure the coming
of spring
to your banks once more.

TAY: *Aye, I know*
that days move by
as daffodils ripple
once crocuses die
and as one colour fades
others invade –
primroses and daisies
buttercups and pansies
adorning
my meadow banks
and riverside gardens,
till russet and gold
repeat the age-old
story of autumn

flaming the trees
to rebellious
displays, so different
from the nature
of my nation
  - one of shy men
  embarrassed of
    revealing passion.

GANGA: And passion is what
          your men have seen
            in my brown depths
            and been afraid of.
          But remember
          my source is
        an icicle cave, colder
        than the north
        of your entire length.
      And I have an extended
      responsibility
    of embracing a
  sub-continent
dependent
on my ability
to drown or drain,
    relying on a capricious sky
      to destroy or sustain
      my millions.

TAY: Your flooded terrain
        left alluvium
        - that loamy compendium
    of silt and sand in which
  my countrymen
  discovered a goldmine
    of crops for gain.
      It is the same
      wanton woman
        you described

earlier, the one
who displaced
the nourishing
loyalty
of rice grains
on your plains.
So your indigenous
corchorus[12]
was planted and
from March to May,
it grew to a glorious
height of ten to twelve
feet in its native domain.
Its yellow flowers
succeeding summer heat,
ready for the reaping
from July till October,
its silky lustre
gathered in bales
of raw jute, heaping
ships waiting
in your Bay
which would later
weave their way
from your port
of Calcutta
to the city
of Dundee
on my banks,
which, in its heyday
was of first rank
and could boast
and give a toast
for being the hub
of the gunny bag club -
its thriving industry.

GANGA: *But that was not*
till the 1830s

when my crops
fed your factories
and Dundee led
the world trade
processing fabrics
from my raw jute –
dull brown sheets
matted from the rubric
of golden yarn –
a success story
spun out in
cinderella splendour.
The near 40,000
hundred weight
of my billowing bales
soared to dizzy heights
of thirteen million
which rose to more
in 1904,
multiplying your sales
beyond speculation
or expectation
as goods from my lands
reached your production arcades
and the rocketing tonnes
linked our strands
by this golden skein.

TAY: *Those massive bales
of 400 pounds
compressed by your
hydraulic power
were processed by
cylinders and teeth
into golden slivers
on my shores;
and later on yours,
toned finer and finer,
with fastidious combs*

then twisted into roves
which, just like our
distributaries, roam
into diverse streams,
the warps with
the hard twist
are swirled
in spools for
dressing and starching
and reeled in hanks
made ready for
bleached futures
and coloured dreams
on factory looms –
active on your shores.
And the wefts –
with the soft twist
were put in neat cops
and thrust
into bags for
weaving
to follow in time.
So there was I
watching your trade
gather momentum,
while I stayed,
biding my time
waiting for the tide
to turn.

GANGA: And it did
with the War
when our jute
had lost
its place as
the golden haired
beauty desired
by the markets
of the West.

The boom of the
pre-War years
tied through
skein and bale
to a world
economy, affected
its market value
as the cost
of production
met reduction
when the course
of the journey
of jute faced
curtailment
with the War
raging along
the jute route.
This tall lass then
had to look to
home-grown devices.
So it was
processed more
and more
on the shores
where it grew.
This tall proud crop
thriving in the damp,
now bowed in defeat
in the world-wide slump
of the demand for jute.

TAY: When prices fell
and the raw jute
lost favour,
I have heard
it plummeted the peasant
of east Bengal
to despair
and the harvesting

cropper
in an oversight
of planters,
was transformed
overnight
to a mendicant
with no
borrowing power.

GANGA: True, his one-time
rice sustaining land
had been turned
to the drenching
might of hemp and strand
of fibrous jute –
crops which now
stood like towers
of impending doom
without the quenching
promise of food.
As famine hit
my lower course
where bumper crops
of rice stood,
they were felled
swiftly, deftly reaped,
and stowed
in stores –
while millions wept
and millions walked
and millions groaned
and died unmourned –
of hunger and fatigue [13]
on my fertile shores.

TAY: I have not witnessed
famine like you,

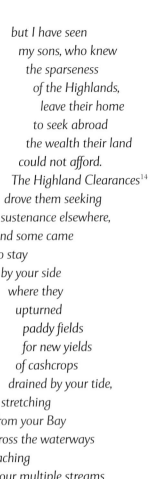

but I have seen
my sons, who knew
the sparseness
of the Highlands,
leave their home
to seek abroad
the wealth their land
could not afford.
The Highland Clearances[14]
drove them seeking
sustenance elsewhere,
and some came
to stay
by your side
where they
upturned
paddy fields
for new yields
of cashcrops
drained by your tide,
stretching
from your Bay
across the waterways
reaching
your multiple streams
and following your length
upwards along the plains
of your alluvial terrain.
So the network
of industries was
assiduously woven,
steadily enmeshing
your shores with mine.
And the golden yarn
still holds with time –
Dundee's factory wheels

and College, for years
have had Bengal's youth
as engineers,
binding technology
with ecology
on your course and mine.

GANGA: Yes, their hopes soared
like rockets freed,
but the great
change that history
decreed
was something
no one had foreseen.
It came with Partition[15]
in a relentless stream
that ruptured
all vision
of a continuous dream.
A line was drawn
on the mindmap of men,
though my waters
refused to be
divided by them.
They created
fresh problems
with the jute
in one land
and the factories
all lined
along another strand –
a curious border
severing the crop
from the machines
that were needed
to process them
for the shops.

TAY: *While here,*
beyond my docks
you will still
find people
who once flocked
to Dundee
when it ruled
the jute trade
in its heyday.
They decided to stay
though the world
turned away
from its flaxen
mainstay –
men who were
unsure
of their next step.

GANGA: *I have heard*
there's a photograph
of sahibs in suits –
all graduates of
Dundee
in a reunion
banquet.
And if you
look closely
at the black and white
shot, you'll see
they are all Indians
hopeful and bright
– a right jovial lot!
But what did they do
when the wheels
stopped dead
with long years
of uncertainty ahead?

TAY: *Right along my*
course and along
diverse banks
of rivers, seacoast and tanks
where people have settled -
the hospitality trade
finds expression in
the finest cuisine
brought from your banks
to mine.
And take it as you may
our Indian restaurants today
are manned and run
by men who came
escaping your sun
and monsoonal rains!
They are mostly from
what is Bangladesh now,
where you are the Padma
and a changeling with
amazing identities.
These men from your Bay
dominate our palate
today
as chicken tikka masala
and creamy korma
become national dishes
of a land from where
the spice wars began.
So the spice route
has turned
a full circle
with Patak and Raj[16]
commemorating
the pinnacle
of easy access
to culinary success.

And other links
have been fostered.
For it just takes
one man
with vision
and synergy
to break
man-made dams.
Patrick Geddes
the town planner
from Ballater
was invited to
design and restore
towns on your shore
which relied
on your tide
and have survived
with pride.

GANGA: I know this man
with his penetrating eyes,
his straggling beard
and leonine mane
that staunchly denied
coercive means
of brush or comb.
I have heard
his footsteps
echo and roam
right down to
Dwasashamedh Ghat[17]
when he touched
my holy water
and imprinted my loam
on a historic visit
to my ancient city.
The powers that ruled,
thought Kashi[18]

too old
  to be preserved
    with its temples
      and palaces,
        its domes
          and its mansions,
        its almhouses
        and resthouses,
        its alleyways
      and byways
    that swerve
  through markets
and sidle down
  to ghats
    built for
      bathing or burning –
        a motley crowd
          of buildings
            that have perched
            for centuries
          with my mandate
          against the furies
        of time and fate.
      This curious blend
    marks my land,
  emblematic
  of civilisation itself,
    a variety, seen in its
      entirety along my journey,
        recognising the existence
          of the rich and the needy
            the grand and the seedy
              side by side –
                and allowed to bide
                with the tolerance
              of an old acceptance.
            And Geddes saw
            the beauty

of Varanasi
as it was,
and decreed
it be untouched
by the bulldozer's
unmitigating crush.
So we owe
Varanasi's presence
to Geddes' essence -
of diagnostic surgery
and restorative sense.

TAY: Geddes grew up
in Perth, which perches
on my shoreline,
moving south after
his birth in Ballater,
that lovely spot
far from my water,
ruled by the Dee
which flows
with easy certainty
to embrace
the icy folds of the
North Sea.
There the bairn
was born,
watched by old oaks
on Craigendarroch,
before he moved on,
when his father
whisked him away
to come and stay
in his gardened world
on my threshold
at Perth, not far from
my birthplace.

GANGA: And where would say
    you really begin –
    near Dochart or Lochay
    or is a loch the place
    of your birth?

TAY: Nay, I would say
    I have an undeclared
    course before they
    call me the Tay.
    Loch Tay lies
    at the source
    of my naming ceremony.
    I will take you in a flashback
    in a retreating dream
    of a back-flowing stream
    on a reverse track.
Before Loch Tay
  I am the Dochart,
   racing over rapids
    from the loch
    of the same name,
    through which I come
    gushing onwards.
    Beyond the Falls
    of Dochart's foam
  I roam as the Fillan,
  carrying on
from Coninish –
  that river which owes
   its flow to the bounty
   of Allt-an-Lund,
    as it tumbles forth
    with energy –
    its birthpangs
    witnessed
    with ecstasy
    from the proud point

of Ben Laoigh,
  the peak
    from where I spring
      in a tumultuous leap
        to journey down
          as Scotland's longest river -
        a picturesque glide
        sliding through
          this high terrain.

GANGA: *It is at Hrishikesh*
          - that sacred place
            where holy men
              meditate and wait
            for benediction -
          that I leap from
        my Himalayan
        heights
      to sweep under
    a precarious
      bridge swinging
        like Lakshman's[19] *temper -*
          a gossamer splendour
            that spans
               my purist freshness,
            where saints gather
          while I begin
        my epic journey
      down the plains
    that know no end

TAY: *I have my*
      bridges too which
        were built
          to conquer
            floods that
              ferries met,
                which swept

the markets
and pavements
of streets
that wept
when my waves
leapt
to scatter
inhabitants.

The floods of 1621
washed away the bridge
that spanned
my course at Perth
and people had
to use the ferry
to sail and carry
men and goods
till 1771,
when another bridge
began this discourse
in stone
that now punctuates
my concourse,
meeting the fleet
of roads
running parallel
to the original
High Street.

Like your Hrishikesh
where sages dwell
I have my Dunkeld
where the saint's
relics were held,
initially called Culdee
and home to a hermit's
Settlement.
But soon the devout
lost interest
when St Andrews won

the relics of their patron
Columbus, to whom they
prayed for protection.

But frequent floods
continued
to deter Scottish
engineers from
providing a fording
means till 1789,
from which time
Dunkeld became
the Highland market
on Fridays.
It is the place
where salmon swam
under Caputh Bridge's span
and the fish
can still float past
the Cathedral which
has reclaimed
Dunkeld's
touristic fame,
its historic walls
enveloped by leafy banks
conscious of my easy stroll.

And at Perth
you will see
marvellous expansions
of bridge on bridge
like multiple
stone visions
that are my epics
in architecture
which defeat
the imagination
that once knew
the floods my waters

could renew
without compunction
or retreat.
The havoc they
could repeat
through the years
with loss of life
and property,
were countered
by constructions
that wiped away
recurrent fears
and the memory
of uncertain
times and tears.

GANGA: *I do know*
your Scottish engineers
as they brought
their spanners
and suspensions,
their cantilevers
and extensions
right across
my expanse
in places where I,
like the sea
stretched on
to eternity –
and only a bridge
once erected
like a rainbow
on sights selected
to define
my boundaries,
made it possible
to imagine
my distant shore.

But nothing
could really confine
my wayward flow.
Mine is a riverine valley
fordable technically,
but my banks
have crumbled
through time
as my waves roll
in serpentine
alternate rhythm,
defying control.
Embankments
and dams
stagger my progress,
with old cities
and new industries,
timeless paddy
and new sprung jute,
which sit side by side
along my route.

And as I leave Patna –
that bastion
of old civilisation
and novel corruption,
I wend south
to assume a sluggish
abandon, branching out
as I reach my mouth
into numerous streams
of brackish water
in the region
of the Mohona.

TAY: *Is this where
the legion city
of Calcutta grew,
born of three villages*

that Job Charnock
drew together
to cradle the trade
of competing commerce?

GANGA: *Kolkata stands*
above the Bay
on one of my
many diversions
- the Hugli.
And along its strand
you can see mansions
beside palaces
and jute bungalows,
which meditate
on this young city's
cosmopolitan reality,
which was once
the second city of Empire.
It has known
renaissance and revolution -
through a chequered history
and now assumes
a new identity
as the cultural capital
of a free country
where the old city
and the new have grown
to encompass and subsume
a hinterland of industry
and suburbs, till it has become
the home to fifteen million
who are proud of its
welcoming intimacy.

TAY: *My Scottish engineers*
once relaxed in your
jute bungalows
after a day's heavy round

of supervising the machines
that churned the returns
on the dusky Hugli which
lapped my memsahibs' world
between Firpo's and Flury's
and tennis parties
before the sun went down
on a way of life
to which your city
owes its birth.

The old and new
sit comfortably
on my banks too.
Looking west from
Dundee you can
spot Newburgh town;
its 18th century
High Street leading
to the tidal mystery
of a once busy
quay with old
fishing boats
encapsulating
its past history –
now embodied
in a sculpture
of a bronze salmon
on a site where
once had stood
a buzzing factory
of imperial activity,
producing linoleum
floor cloth, bound
to the jute grown
on your home ground.
Today a park
and new housing
spill over and fill

the place that once
supplied 700 jobs
over a hundred years
till as late
as 1978.

GANGA: I meet my present
and my past
at Prayag,[20]
that holy raag[21]
of harmony –
my Triveni[22]
where my living
sister Jamuna
spills her arms
of loving pearls
and we remember
one lost stream,
a sister who
survives in dreams,
the Saraswati
who still runs
in the portals
of earth's wombs.

And it is here that Motilal[23]
saw his son
grow up to spurn
a life under
a foreign yoke
that he with
Gandhi
strove to break
and revoke
the dignity
of living free
beside
my abiding tide.

TAY: *I too have known*
the tedium
of being confined
by a union
that blurred
the reality
of individuality
for my nation,
subsumed
by the history
of a debated quartet,
and allowed to
resume
its identity
as the land
of Adam Smith
and David Hume
in a peaceful revolution
of devolution.

GANGA: *I have known*
revolution
of another kind
in a Land
Reform Movement
igniting young minds
with the spark
of bringing improvement
through annihilation
of old institutions.[24]
It was quenched
with brute force
but it is still not
a lost voice,
though driven underground,
smouldering
in villages
that I sustain,
as folk

fight back in a
final struggle
for prime land
for which they
see no substitution
in spite of
industrialisation.
This struggle
with the government
began two decades
after your people
had transferred power
to mine, and the
memory of Empire
had become a faded
reality as new wars
invaded my weeping
embankments.

TAY: But looking back,
when my men
and women
mingled with yours,
through years
of imperial association –
those centuries[25]
have not been
without gain
for my men
who filled
the cornchest
of Scotland[26]
with grain
and yarn
gleaned and grown
on your hot land.
They came back
with memories
and longings

nurtured and nourished
in times made irrelevant
by war's devastation
as a generation
was left to pick up
the pieces after the Blitz.
So the returned
expatriates
could only cherish
and ruminate
on a life
they had known
in the private chambers
of their mind and home.

GANGA: I know this agony
of longing, as some
of your countrymen
remained on my shore –
the only one they knew,
made familiar and true
through custom and time
where they had spent
their prime
and would continue
to drink
their whisky sodas
as dusk enveloped
their verandahs.

But the old life was gone
and a new
constitution brought
fresh dreams
of a nation, eager
to see fiefdoms
and kingdoms,
plantations and palaces
become chapters

of an old book
of imperial history.
Democracy
demanded a new
resolution
of, albeit,
a truncated entity
in the identity
of two nations
fulfilling a pledge
with destiny.[27]
recovering
though not in full measure
but very substantially -
in a tryst with time[28]
which cut up their land
and their people
in a wrench that tore
minds, [29]but
could not succeed
in ripping my waters
or carving boundaries
on my fluid freedom -
so they continue
to debate
about ownership
and demarcation,
the possibility
of amalgamation
as remote as the
Himalayan peaks -
of my initiation route.
So I enfold their seed,
feed their
multiplying breed
and from time to time
I drown them
in seasonal spate

that has its beginnings
on the very brink
of my banks.

TAY: *Yes, men have*
not discovered that
the earth creates
her own natural
borders
which they cannot
decide
even when they call for
boundaries
along ethnic divides
which spill over
courses that we will
continue to run
as nature decrees –
not men.

There will always
be the old life
folded in the new.
It is for me and you
to nurture
what we value
within our banks
and close our ranks
to protect
and save
the treasures
of our waves.

GANGA: *And what can we do*
when another revolution
alters our riviera
beyond recognition?
Tourists today
may take a launch
and glide down

my branch
  on the Hugli
    by day.
      And the city
        of palaces[30]
          with edifices
            of grandeur
              will unravel
                in a sprawl
                  that will enthral
                  the viewer.
              And what can
            be newer
          than the fresh
        development
      that overpowers
    and denies
      a whole age
        of achievement
          against the jute
            managers' bungalows
            standing in mute
            testimony to old times
          as old mills
          stay silent
            on the reflective
            embankment.

TAY: But unlike men
      whose riches know
      rise and fall
    with time's flow –
  we have our riches,
  which we hold
    in our folds
      as we ride
        high or subside –
        treasures that
        we cherish

unlike they who destroy
what they have today
for instant gain,
without thought of
tomorrow's pain.
So in my
ever-flowing stream
I have always
harboured dreams
that I will now
share with you.

From Perth
to Dunkeld
I have borne
and proudly held
shoals of salmon
who have swum
against my current
and ultimately won
a strenuous race
claiming their
territory finally
from me,
journeying upstream
from the dark pools
where they lay
waiting. There the
anglers came by day
to drop their lines
and catch their prey,
which in time
had dwindled drastically
to their dismay
and that of gourmets
who today find
the salmon of the wild
replaced by the child

of hatcheries in farms.
For my tributaries
are seeded now
with the view
to multiply the few -
ensuring huge runs of fish
up the Almond
to the lower beats
in March, the middle
beats in May, reaching
the upper beats
on mild July days.
Noticeable numbers
swim to Ericht
but there is no
direct gain for me
as they say
the Tay
is the last
gasping foothold
for the stragglers
who find their way
to my headwaters
at the end of the day -
repeating an old
journey,
but having lost
the adventurous
boldness
of the past,
the pleasure
of being born
in the wilderness
when nature reigned
before nurture drained
the will to breed free
in utmost liberty
from poaching distress.

GANGA: *You call your salmon*
the gourmet fish.
I too have one
to match
your favoured dish.
It too is
an estuary fish –
the silver hilsa
which swims close
to the Bay.
And when the Monsoons
come, it makes
its way upstream
to spawn along
my distributaries –
the Rupnarayan
the Bhagirathi
the Hugli,
and in my surging sister
the turbulent Padma.
But now the hilsa
is facing disaster
as greedy fishing
jeopardises
my stock of this
merchandise.

TAY: *I have known*
such disasters
when Russian
ships netted
my free waters
for the sand eels
that my salmon
feed on.
And well-meaning
friends
of the environment
have saved the seals

that make a meal
of my salmon
the gourmet fish
that is sure
to diminish
if the Scots
are now not
canny enough
to devise means
to replenish
the shoals
and cherish
and protect
the numbers
that still
fill my stream
which has been
their ancient home.

GANGA: *In deltaic Bengal*
where I drift
into multiple identities
in a mesh of waterways
that know swift
changeability in flash
floods upstream, which
then affect my layout
on a whim,
where I am not
what I seem,
flowing at ease
apparently mellowed
in my twilight course,
but finding the old
individualism
and spark
in the turbulent
diversion of the Padma
- the intractable

unpredictable -
surging or calm
destructive or creative,
her vibrant depths
the ultimate home
of the proverbial
delicacy, the seasonal
Hilsa of Bengal.

TAY: And is your hilsa
still at home
and teeming
in your generous
stream?
Heavy trawling
in the open sea
of diverse shoals
has put pressure
on the salmon
stocks in me.

GANGA: My fishermen
fish in small boats,
as trawlers are
beyond their means.
But I have
another curse.
The industries along
my banks
and all the cities
who belong
to my course
spew their fumes,
their filth and waste
that through the years
have consumed
my strength
and goodness,
and I can trace

the threatening line
that brings decline
to the hilsa's race.
The pollution
makes them gasp
for breath
in my depths
as fish grow still
under the weight
of the mill
of modernity's will
and fear of death.

TAY: I have had
some gracious schemes
to clear my banks
and clean my streams.
Have you had
some men
of vision
with a similar mission
and drive
to revive
your tired flow?

GANGA: True. I've had
my share
of programmes
for my water's care -
'The Ganga Development
Project.' It has begun
in stages to reclaim
my sacrosanct
name and fame.

TAY: In this day
and age
you can't be
serious and sage

when you say
that your waves
are held as sacred
today.

GANGA: *In this country*
a river's history
has spiritual grace -
it is born in heaven
and carries divine force
in its wayward course.

And none is more sacred
than my flowing water
and every drop of it
is blessed matter
for the believer.
To drink from me
is to be cleansed
from sins' fury.
Drops from me
bring true shanti
on heads bowed
in worship and piety
to my deity.
All along my length
people wade in it
at dawn and sunset
to feel my strength
and see the dark fade
and pray for the light
to return at my side.
Lamps are floated
with flames that quiver
up and down the
length of my river
and petals are scattered
for my intervention
with the mighty Shiva.

TAY: *It's a different world here*
where the spiritual stays clear
amidst a reality
that is bracing and braw
and myths seem remote
as my waters promote
all the sports
of racing that draw
the sportsmen
in Scotsmen
as the river offers
challenges
of braving the blast –
and the Scots who
once held the mast
of shipping
and trading,
now find expression
in skimming my surge
with adventurous urge –
so my white-water rapids
are the heady delight
of rafters and canoeists
watched from heights
of the hills that contemplate
my course.
The excitement of movement
on the splurge of my waves
is far from what your
countrymen meditate
as they watch your force.
The clock has turned
in a fresh resolution
as paragliding
and yachting,
kayaking and canoeing
provide the adventure
that once drew men

to venture
across the ocean

GANGA: But they do return
            as English binds
             the globalised –
              and they come
               to join a new
                network, not of rivers
                but of the web
               which weaves them
              into the folds
             of my old cities
            where India's
           young dare
          to dream
         of a universe
        speaking across
       time and space
      as one half sleeps
       and another awakes
        aware of the divisions
         of a weapon building world
          of political suspicion.

TAY: I think
          we stand
           on the brink
            of disaster
             that spells danger
              for our future
               if trident missiles
                are guarded and improved,
               not destroyed or removed,
                for they will annihilate
                 the human race
                  from the face
                   of this planet.
                    Our defence

is our resilience -
an ability
to accept change
and learn
to move on
as we range
through old routes
embracing the possibilities
of newfound
diversity.

Yours is a culture
my people sought,
looking for spiritualism
when smothered by
the materialism
they bought so easily
in lands where the sun set
and families felt fractured
by the tide
of individualism.

GANGA: We seem to have turned
from that symbol
of equanimity
we once offered,
enveloped now
in a climate
of nurtured hate
and anticipated
enmity -
for my country went
delirious some years ago
when it exploded fission bombs
to set alight a chain reaction
in neighbouring Pakistan.
And then with Afghanistan
becoming a place for
bombing revelry

and with one death in
 five of every Iraqi alive,
  my people feel smugly
   safe from invasion
    and occupation.
     Yet what they fail
      to comprehend
       is that storing nuclear
        warheads
         can only guarantee more dead
          created the foundation of
           suspicion and dread
            which trigger new
             explosions that punctuate
city lives
 living under
  the uncertain shadow
   of an inexplicable hate.

TAY: You and I can only do
      what we do best,
       that is flow with the
        certainty of continuity –

GANGA: Letting our water's
          sacred truth seep into
           human consciousness
            as the source of life
             like light and trees,
              the earth and breeze –

    TAY: Our rhythms
          spelling harmony,
           which, if nurtured,
            can guarantee
            Shanti[31] for eternity.

Notes

1. Also known as the Ganges in English.

2. According to Hinduism, there is one God, the Absolute who has many manifestations. So there is the Hindu Trinity with Bramha the Creator, Vishnu the Preserver and Shiva the Destroyer. Shiva sits on Mount Kailash, in trance-like meditation. But when there is a sinful world, he wakes up and in a dance of destruction – the *tandava* – destroys it, and over the ashes of the old, Bramha creates a new world, which Vishnu preserves.

3. Thor is the Nordic god of thunder. Born of Odin and Jord, he is the most powerful of gods and is married to the goddess of fertility, Sif. Like Odin, Thor is always portrayed as a large, strong man. But while Odin is depicted as a tall, middle-aged man with a long beard and one eye, Thor is distinguished for his red beard and lightning eyes.

4. Odin is the god of wisdom, war and death. His parents are the giants Borr and Bestla. He is also revered as the god of magic, poetry, prophecy and hunting. He wears a grey cloak with a blue hood.

5. The Himalayas, the highest and youngest fold mountains in the world.

6. A section of the Himalayas.

7. The Bhagirati river originates in the Gangotri glacier in the Himalayas, which merges with Alaknanda river after 700 miles. It is after this that the river is called the Ganga. There is another distributary of the Ganga called the Bhagirati-Hugli in its lower reaches.

8. Makara is Capricorn, Ganga's carrier.

9. The source of the Ganga.

10. Both Jadganda and Kshurganga are tributaries of the Ganga.

11. Literally, *godhuli* refers to the dust (*dhuli*) raised by the cows' (*go*) hooves as they return at dusk.

12. The corchorus belongs to the family of Malvaceae, native to tropical and subtropical regions. It is an annual with yellow flowers, growing tall to a height of 2–4 meters. The fibre produced from it is jute.

13. A reference to the man-made famine of Bengal in 1943, when millions died.

14. The Highland Clearances took place in the 18th century. Landlords cleared the Scottish Highlands of subsistence farmers, resulting in the displacement of many people and a whole way of life.

15. In August 1947, India was Partitioned to form the new nation which comprised of West Pakistan and East Pakistan. While Pakistan came into being on 14 August 1947, India became independent on 15 August 1947. In 1971, East Pakistan became Bangladesh.

16. Patak and Raj are two popular brands in Britain which make spice mixtures.

17. Ghat is the landing stage on a river, the wharf or quay; the brick or stone steps leading to a lake or pond. Dwasashamedh Ghat is in Benares.

18. Kashi is another name for Varanasi or Benares.

19. Lakshman is known for his unswerving loyalty to his brother Rama and Rama's wife, Sita, and his quick temper is proverbial as he protects Rama and Sita jealously. Rama is the hero of the Hindu epic, *The Ramayana*.

20. Prayag is the old name for Allahabad.

21. *Raag* or *raga* in Indian classical music, is the melodic pattern which is the basis for improvisation.

22. Triveni is the meeting point of three rivers.

23. Motilal Nehru is Jawaharlal Nehru's father. The latter was the first Prime Minister of Independent India in 1947 till 1964.

24. A reference to the Naxalite Movement that began in the late '60s, was broken with a heavy hand through police intervention in the mid '70s, but goes on as a resistance movement in many rural areas, especially in Bihar.

25. The first British ship landed in Surat, India in 1608.

26. A description of India by Sir Walter Scott.

27. An echo of Nehru's speech on the eve of Indian Independence, 'A Tryst with Destiny'.

28. Ibid.

29. A reference to the Indian Partition.

30. Calcutta (now Kolkata), is known as the city of palaces.

31. The Sanskrit word for peace, which is common to many Indian languages.

List of Illustrations

PAGE

12 Old Calcutta, courtesy of Anne Morell

14 *Left*: East India Co Coin (half anna), 1835
    Right: Reverse of coin with Urdu inscription:
      'With this you can have what you desire.'
    Centre: Courtesy of the Black Watch Museum, Perth (KM)

15 *Top right*: Ganga leaving the Himalayas (BF)
    Bottom right: Crannog on Loch Tay (KM)

16 *Top left*: Looking west from Perth (KM)
    Bottom left: Lord Shiva (BF)

17 *Top right*: The meditative Ganga (BF)
    Bottom right: Newburgh by Mugdrum Island (KM)

18 *Top left*: Evergreen sculpture pillar, Perth (KM)
    Bottom left: River Tay at Perth (KM)

19 *Top right*: The meandering Ganga (BF)
    Bottom right: Balmerino Abbey (KM)

20 *Top left*: Homage to Ganga (BF)
    Bottom left: Waves (BF)

21 *Top right*: Homage of a populace (BF)
    Bottom right: Capricious flow (BF)

22 *Top left*: Rafting at Aberfeldy (KM)
    Bottom left: Ferry boats on the Ganga (KM)

23 *Top left*: The land the Ganga drains (BF)
    Middle right: Yellow rapeseed (KM)

24 *Bottom left*: Day has broken (BF)
    Bottom right: Reverence (BF)

25 *Top right*: Morning prayers at Varanasi (KM)
    Bottom right: Ancient tributary at Varanasi (KM)

26 *Middle left*: 'Bengal' detail from headstone in Perth (KM)
    Bottom left: River Tay sign (KM)

27 *Top right*: Angling by the Tay (KM)
    Bottom right: Ferry family at Varanasi (KM)

28 *Top left*: When the sun reigns (BF)
    Bottom left: Durga Puja

29   Ferry Boat stone (KM)

30   *Middle left*: *Sonar Tori*, The Golden Boat (KM)
      Bottom left: Daffodils at Aberfeldy bridge & raft (KM)

31   *Middle left*: Embracing a sub-continent (BF)
      Middle right: Visitors from the North (KM)

32   Boat waiting (KM)

33   *Top right*: Red sail: *Sonar Tori* (KM)
      Middle right: Howrah Bridge (BF)

34   Tay Bridge to Dundee (KM)

35   *Top right*: The God of War, Lakshman – Rama's Defender (BF)
      Bottom right: The jute route (BF)

36   *Top left*: Silvery Tay (KM)
      Bottom left: The Second Hugli Bridge (KM)

37   *Top right*: Cliffs of Kinnoul Perth (KM);
      Bottom left: At the Dundee Verdant Jute Museum (KM)

38   *Middle left*: The condluence of a moving population (BF)
      Bottom right: Newburgh stone boat (KM)

39   *Top right*: Family fishing near Kirkton (KM)
      Bottom left: Along the bank (BF)

40   Settling on the banks (BF)

41   *Top right*: Geddes and students
      Bottom right: Ducks at Varanasi (KM)

42   *Top left*: Pillars at Varanasi (KM)
      Bottom left: Temple at Varanasi (KM)

43   *Top right*: Stained glass commissioned by Geddes (KM)
      Bottom right: Loch Tay (KM)

44   *Top left*: Falls (KM)
      Bottom left: Balmerino Abbey (KM)

45   *Top right*: Lakshman Jhula at Hrishikesh (BF)
      Bottom right: Bridges and floods

46   Dunkeld Cathedral (KM)

47   Perth Bridge (BF)

48   The Bridge (BF)

49   Bengal Plains (KM)

50   *Top left*: On the Hugli (BF)
     Bottom left: In Dock, Dundee; courtesy Dundee City Council (KM)

51   Newburgh (KM)

52   *Top left*: At Prayag (BF)
     Bottom left: Anand Bhavan at Allahabad (BF)

53   A population adrift (BF)

54   *Top left*: Love boats (KM)
     Bottom left: Scottish Cemetery (KM)

55   In the gardens of today (BF)

56   Fluid freedom (BF)

57   Newburgh boats (KM)

58   Tay Bridge at Dunkeld (KM)

59   Pensive angler near Bottom Craig (KM)

60   The catch of the Monsoons (KM)

61   *Top right*: Pictish salmon (KM)
     Bottom right: Meigle stone fish (KM)

62   *Middle right*: At the edge of the Sunderbans (BF)
     Bottom left: Durga, the victorious (KM)

63   *Top right*: *Sonar Tori*, now in Scottish Maritime Museum (KM)
     Bottom right: The day's catch (KM)

64   *Top left*: Indian paper boats (KM)
     Bottom left: Holy water (BF)

65   *Top left*: Spiritual grace (BF)
     Middle right: Floating lamp and prayers (BF)
     Bottom left: Pensive light (BF)

66   *Top left*: Waking to new dreams (BF)
     Bottom left: Rafting on the Tay (KM)

67   Kinnoul Hill Folly (KM)

68   Zooming over sacred waters (BF)

69   Bridge for peace (BF)

Tartan and Turban

Bashabi Fraser

ISBN 1 84282 044 3   PBK   £8.99

Let the powder clouds of Holi –
the festival of colour – cover you in
purple, pink and green.

Be mesmerised by the proud
hooded cobra weaving its charm.

Join a wedding wrapped up in
reams of yellow silk and incense
and alive with the swish of green
kilts and the sound of bagpipes.

Watch the snow melt on the crest
of soft dawns and feel the slash of
rain against your numb cheek as
the wind races across from the
North Sea.

Read Bashabi Fraser's poetry and
experience a swirl of emotions and
images.

A Bengali poet living in Scotland,
Bashabi Fraser creatively spans the
different worlds she inhabits,
celebrating the contrasts of the
two countries whilst also finding
commonality. Focusing on clear
themes and issues – displacement,
removal, belonging, identity, war –
her poetry is vibrant with feeling
and comes alive in an outrageous
game of sound patterns.

... mixes up some extraordinarily tasty
Indian rhythms with eloquent, Saltire-
phile verse.
THE LIST

Tartan & Turban *pulses with*
youthful vitality that invites readers to
partake of her hospitality, as she
mischievously pokes fun at language

tartan
& turban

'Here is an exotic Bengali flower,
transplanted in auld Edina.'
ROBERT ALAN JAMIESON

BASHABI FRASER

and the vagaries of her Indo-Scot
migrant existence within this well-
structured collection. Fraser elegantly
dances between the first- and second-
generation cultural perspectives, as her
enthusiastic writing takes us from
West Bengal to London to the
Highlands of Scotland.
WASAUTH 49

Stolen from Africa

Kokumo Rocks
ISBN 1 906307 19 9 PBK £7.99

Have you ever seen a megalomaniac butterfly throw a hissy fit?

Ever been mown down by a disgruntled lawnmower?

Run from a bully? Have you ever noticed that there are no black prosthetic legs?

Kokumo Rock's poetry is a vibrant and energetic foray into a world of absurd situations and vivid imagination. Drawing on all the senses, she expresses anger over war, joy in the natural world, and delights in the silly and strange aspects of life.

While Kokumo expresses her despair over racism and war, she will convey, in the next moment, the joyful suggestion of a better future. You will laugh at the way she brings life and energy to everyday objects and, above all, relish the refreshing and passionate poetry of Scotland's dynamic African-Asian performance poet as she celebrates and examines her own background.

Kokumo's unique humour permeates the entire collection, endowing her strong political message with an irresistible sense of humanity and humour.

... similar to Angelou's work, but sharper and more hip.
SHEREEN TUOMI

Bad Ass Raindrop

Kokumo Rocks
ISBN 1 84282 018 4 PBK £6.99

What would happen if a raindrop took acid?

Does your bum shake and does your belly wobble?

And have you noticed that there are no black babies on 'New Baby' cards?

Fadeke Kokumo Rocks' poetry is alive with love, passion, humour and brutal honesty. It is sharply observed, potent and insightful, capturing beautifully the sixth dimension of the creative eye. It has a rich diversity of time and content, which embraces the globe and its conflicts, domestic and urban.

You can hear the monsoon rains of Africa, taste the mangoes of India, touch the compassion and spirit of the child and sense the pain of burning flesh as race riots rage.

Read the eclectic, electrifying poetry of Kokumo Rocks in this collection containing over 30 of her most popular poems. Full of Kokumo's distinctive humour, *Bad Ass Raindrop* challenges the questions we answer unquestioning.

Bodywork

Dilys Rose

ISBN 1 905222 93 9 PBK £8.99

How do we feel about the flesh that surrounds us and how do we deal with the knowledge that it will eventually do so no more? How do our bodies affect our emotional, physical and spiritual lives?

Winner of the 2006 McCash prize, Dilys Rose's third collection of poetry focuses on the human body in all its glory, comedy and frailty; on the quirks, hazards and conundrums of physiology; on intimations of mortality – and immortality. Rose draws fully-grown characters in a few vivid strokes; from a body double to a cannibal queen, their souls are personified in a limb, affliction or skill. These poems get under your skin and into your bones – you'll never look at the human body in the same way again!

Dilys Rose exposes and illuminates humanity with scalpel sharpness... ingeniously exciting, quirky and perceptive.
Janet Paisley, THE SCOTSMAN

It's an extraordinary book, brave and unusual, full of unexpected insights and delights – and a consistent compassion, respect and reverence for the human body, in all its oddity and complexity.
CATHERINE SMITH

On the Flyleaf

Ken Cockburn

ISBN 1 906307 18 0 PBK £7.99

... Its flyleaves are thick

with poems: Sophus Claussen, you explain, those you didn't know by heart and wishing,

one long-ago summer, to travel light, copied in the space Calvino offered.

Art, sex, a city, a journey: Ken Cockburn's new collection dwells on the connection between people, places, languages and literature. Inspired by inscriptions, graffiti and scribbled notes on the flyleaves of books – Ovid, a guide book, a superhero comic – these poems interweave travel, home and love, while quietly subverting notions of standing and rank in literature.

Handling both the narrative poem and the haiku with equal skill, Cockburn observes and probes the ways in which we interpret the world with an uncluttered eye.

Fascinating well-wrought contemporary poems... exact and apparently effortless writing.
ANGUS REID

100 Favourite Scottish Poems

Edited by Stewart Conn
ISBN 1 905222 61 0 PBK £7.99

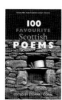

Poems to make you laugh. Poems to make you cry. Poems to make you think. Poems to savour. Poems to read out loud. To read again, and again. Scottish poems. Old favourites. New favourites. 100 of the best. Scotland has a long history of producing outstanding poetry. From the humblest but-and-ben to the grandest castle, the nation has a great tradition of celebration and commemoration through poetry. *100 Favourite Scottish Poems* – incorporating the top 20 best-loved poems as selected by a BBC Radio Scotland listener poll – ranges from ballads to Burns, from 'Proud Maisie' to 'The Queen of Sheba', and from 'Cuddle Doon' to 'The Jeelie Piece Song'.

Brainheart

Paraig MacNeil
ISBN 1 905222 31 9 PBK £6.99

What Scottish slave abolished black slavery in Morocco in the 18th century?

How did a journalist invent the kaleidoscope?

What was the name of the first pony-pulled lawnmower?

Disguised as a Chinese boy, what Scotsman brought tea to the British Empire?

Paraig MacNeil takes a unique and quirky look at the age of innovation, reflecting on what Scottish inventors, politicians and good Samaritans have offered the world, from the steam train and drainage guttering, to marmalade and the light bulb.

MacNeil offers a brief introduction to each innovator followed by a heroic eulogy based on the style of 'Blind Harry's Wallace', the epic poem praising William Wallace's heroic deeds.

The journey into the age of invention is a light-hearted one and lets the reader revel in the inspiring creativity of 50 Scottish men and women. MacNeil successfully and cleverly fuses verbal wit with a short history of Scottish innovation.

Luath Press Limited
committed to publishing well written books worth reading

LUATH PRESS takes its name from Robert Burns, whose little collie Luath (*Gael.,* swift or nimble) tripped up Jean Armour at a wedding and gave him the chance to speak to the woman who was to be his wife and the abiding love of his life. Burns called one of 'The Twa Dogs' Luath after Cuchullin's hunting dog in *Ossian's Fingal*. Luath Press was established in 1981 in the heart of Burns country, and is now based a few steps up the road from Burns' first lodgings on Edinburgh's Royal Mile. Luath offers you distinctive writing with a hint of unexpected pleasures.

Most bookshops in the UK, the US, Canada, Australia, New Zealand and parts of Europe either carry our books in stock or can order them for you. To order direct from us, please send a £sterling cheque, postal order, international money order or your credit card details (number, address of cardholder and expiry date) to us at the address below. Please add post and packing as follows: UK – £1.00 per delivery address; overseas surface mail – £2.50 per delivery address; overseas airmail – £3.50 for the first book to each delivery address, plus £1.00 for each additional book by airmail to the same address. If your order is a gift, we will happily enclose your card or message at no extra charge.

Luath Press Limited
543/2 Castlehill
The Royal Mile
Edinburgh EH1 2ND
Scotland
Telephone: 0131 225 4326 (24 hours)
Fax: 0131 225 4324
email: sales@luath.co.uk
Website: www.luath.co.uk